My First Reference Book About

Food

Contents

Food

Illustrated by Rosalinde Bonnet

Written by Felicity Brooks
and Hannah Wood

Designed by Francesca Allen
and Kirsty Tizzard

American Editor: Carrie Armstrong

How vegetables grow

Vegetables grow in or under the soil. Some are the roots, stems, bulbs or flowers of plants.

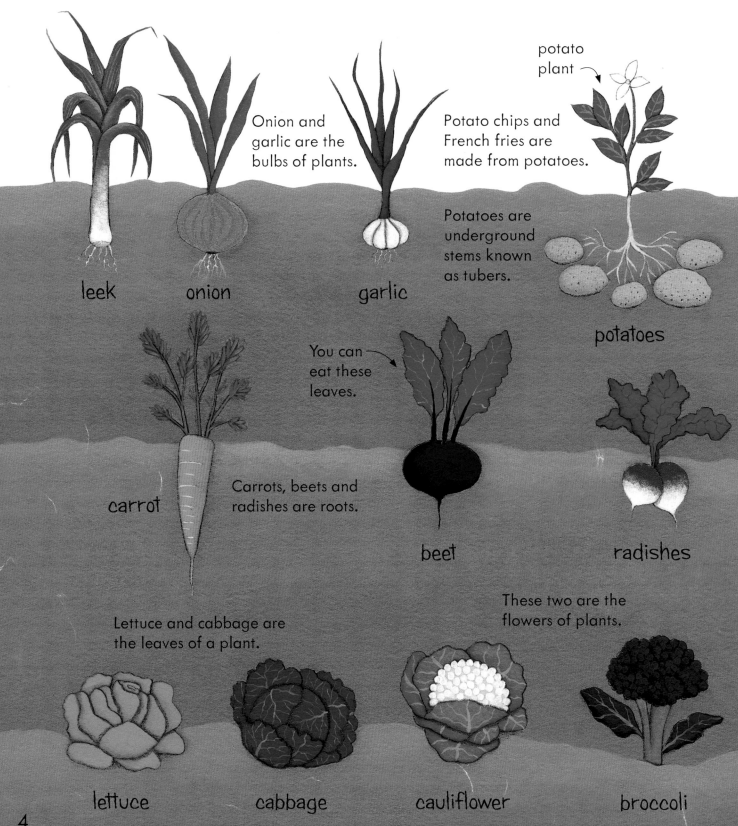

Onion and garlic are the bulbs of plants.

potato plant

Potato chips and French fries are made from potatoes.

Potatoes are underground stems known as tubers.

leek

onion

garlic

potatoes

You can eat these leaves.

carrot

Carrots, beets and radishes are roots.

beet

radishes

These two are the flowers of plants.

Lettuce and cabbage are the leaves of a plant.

lettuce

cabbage

cauliflower

broccoli

You can grow most vegetables from seeds.
They need sunshine and water, and some
time to grow.

How many of
these vegetables
do you know?

turnip

artichoke

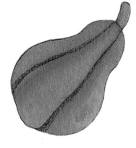

butternut squash

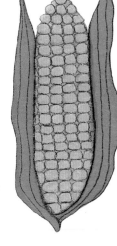

corn

pod

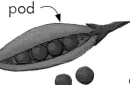

peas

cucumber

celery

pepper

green beans

spinach

asparagus

mushroom

okra

zucchini

parsnip

endive

Brussels sprout

sweet potato

kale

5

Fruits of the world

Fruit grows on trees, bushes and plants.
Which of these fruits have you tried?

apple

pear

cherries

plum

peach

banana

orange

mango

grapefruit

apricot

lemon

lime

grapes

raspberry

strawberry

Lots of fruit trees
grow together in
an orchard.

pear trees

apple tree

Jam jar puzzle

Jam is often made from soft fruits such as plums and berries.

a)

b)

c)

d)

Can you guess which fruits these jams are made of? (Answers on page 32.)

pineapple

melon

pumpkin

These are fruits, but you can eat them as vegetables.

eggplant

tomato

apple tree

tractor

beehive

plum tree

fruit-picker

Milk and dairy foods

These four foods are called dairy products.
They are all made from milk.

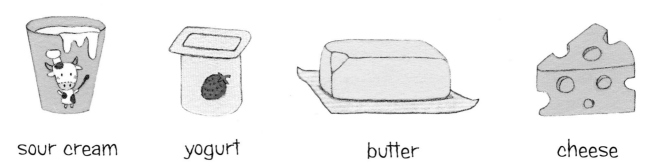

sour cream   yogurt   butter   cheese

Most milk comes from cows. They go to a milking
shed each day so the farmer can milk them.

milking machine   farmer

A truck called a milk tanker
takes the milk from the farm
to a place called a dairy.

At the dairy the milk is heated
to kill germs. Then it is put into
bottles or cartons to sell.

A choice of cheese

Many different kinds of cheeses are made from cow's milk. Which do you like to eat?

Blue mold gives this a strong taste.

This hard skin is called rind.

stilton

parmesan

soft and lumpy

cottage cheese

camembert

holes

emmental

Monterey Jack

These cheeses are made from sheep's or goat's milk.

goat's cheese

manchego

ricotta

feta

goat

sheep

All about eggs

Most of the eggs that we eat come from hens. Hens lay their eggs in a henhouse or barn.

rooster

henhouse

hens

eggs

Chicks are baby hens.

chick

You can eat eggs from ducks and geese, too. Their eggs are bigger than hens' eggs.

duck

goose

basket

Farmers collect the eggs and put them in boxes to sell.

How to break an egg

Hold the egg in one hand. Tap it firmly on the rim of a bowl.

Put your thumbs into the crack and pull the shell apart.

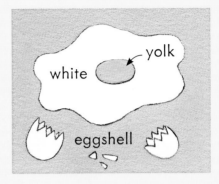

white · yolk · eggshell

Let the clear 'white' and the yellow yolk slide into the bowl.

How do you like your eggs?

These children like eggs cooked in different ways. Which do you like best?

Fried egg, please!

Scrambled egg for me.

I like my eggs hard-boiled.

You can buy eggs in special cartons or trays.

Where meat comes from

Most meat comes from animals that live on farms.

Pork comes from pigs.

pig

Beef comes from cows.

cows

sheep

lamb

Lamb comes from young sheep.

Turkey meat comes from turkeys.

Chicken meat comes from chickens.

Duck meat comes from ducks.

turkey

chicken

duck

At the meat counter

A butcher cuts meat up to sell. Meat has to be cooked before you can eat it.

pork loin

lamb chops

ground beef

All these kinds of foods are made from meat.

sausages

ham

burgers

meatballs

salami

bacon

Baking bread and cakes

Bread is made mostly of flour.
Flour is usually made from a
kind of grass called wheat that
farmers grow in fields.

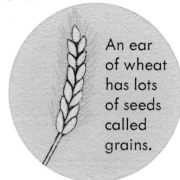

An ear
of wheat
has lots
of seeds
called
grains.

Grains of wheat are
ground up into a fine
powder to make flour.

Yeast makes
dough rise.

yeast

Bakers mix flour, yeast,
water and salt together
to make a dough.

oven

kneading

They knead the dough,
let it rise, shape it and
bake it in an oven.

Different kinds of bread

Have you ever noticed how many
different kinds of bread there are?
Have you tried any of these?

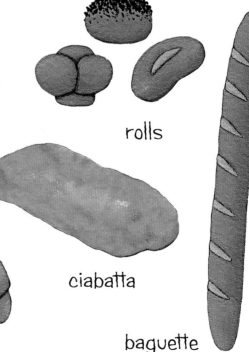

rolls

ciabatta

baguette

Flat breads don't
have yeast in them.

tin loaf

pita

croissant

Cake competition

Bakers make cakes from flour, butter, sugar and eggs. Then they add other flavors and toppings. These beautiful cakes are in a baking competition.

Simon's strawberry cake

Charlotte's chiffon cake

Grace's gâteau

Lucy's layer cake

Charlie's chocolate tower

Cathy's cupcakes

You can be the judge and choose which cakes should get 1st, 2nd and 3rd prize.

Fresh fish and seafood

Most fish live wild in rivers, lakes and the sea, but some fish that we eat come from fish farms.

fishing boat

Fish live in water and people use nets or fishing rods to catch them.

fisherman

net

All these fish live in the sea.

cod

flounder

haddock

tuna

mackerel

sardine

salmon

All sorts of seafood

There are lots of other things from the sea that you can eat. They are called seafood.

shrimp

crab

squid

octopus

lobster

oysters

clams

mussels

If you look at a fish counter, you can see different kinds of fish and seafood.

Fran's Fish

red mullet

salmon

smoked haddock

clams

scallops

What is pasta?

Pasta is made from a kind of wheat flour mixed with eggs or water and salt.

To make pasta, you mix eggs with flour and salt to form a dough.

Then you roll the dough out until it is very thin and cut it into shapes.

A pasta machine can help you roll the pasta out thinly and shape it.

You can buy all kinds of pasta shapes to cook. Pasta comes from Italy, so the shapes have Italian names.

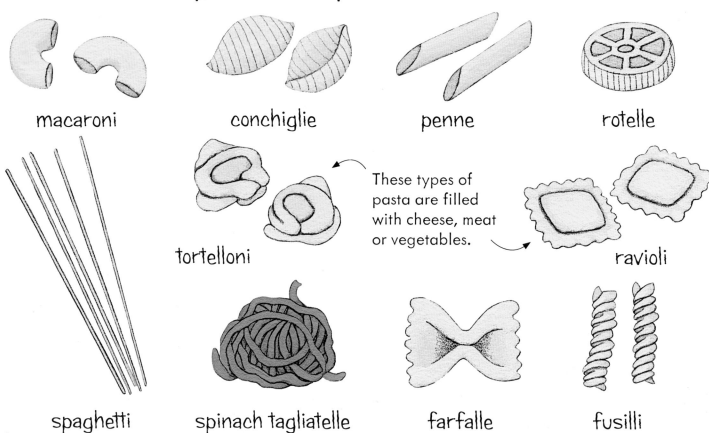

macaroni

conchiglie

penne

rotelle

tortelloni

These types of pasta are filled with cheese, meat or vegetables.

ravioli

spaghetti

spinach tagliatelle

farfalle

fusilli

18

How we get rice

Rice grows on plants. There are more than 8,000 kinds. Most grow best in shallow water in hot countries.

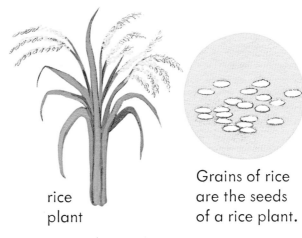
rice plant

Grains of rice are the seeds of a rice plant.

These are some of the things that can be made from rice. Have you tried any?

puffed rice cereal

sushi

risotto

rice cakes

paella

Rice farmers stand in the water to cut down rice plants so they can collect the grains.

Rice fields are known as paddy fields.

At the market

This market sells all the foods you have found out about in this book. Which stall would you visit first?

Matt's Meat

Frankie's Fruit

Claire's Cakes

Vera's Vegetables

Fran's Fish

Paolo's Pasta

Brenda's Bread

Where do you keep it?

You can buy food in a ...

tub   tube   carton   bottle

can   package   box   jar

Cans, jars and packages can go in a pantry.
Fresh food needs to be kept in the refrigerator.

pantry

refrigerator

Cooking words

wash

peel

chop

grate

roll

mix

pour

beat

weigh

fry

pan

pot

rolling pin

scales

spatula

whisk

wooden spoon

knife

chopping board

bowl

grater

colander

Making meals

Here are some meals and snacks you could make from the foods in this book. Which do you like best?

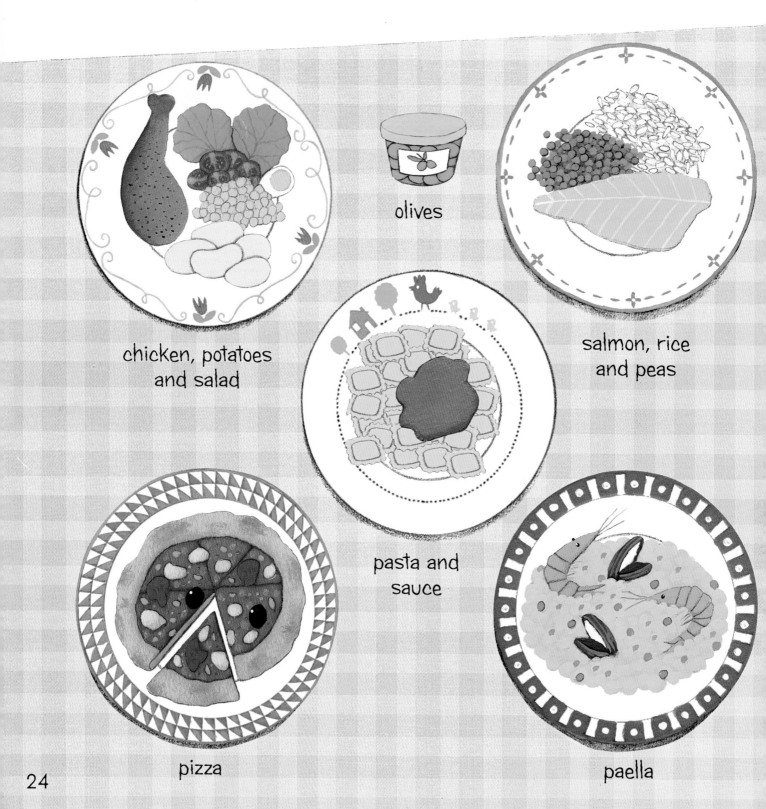

olives

chicken, potatoes and salad

salmon, rice and peas

pasta and sauce

pizza

paella

Yum, yum, sausage!

jam

sausage, French fries and baked beans

breaded fish, mashed potatoes and broccoli

croissants

fresh fruit

ice cream

meatballs and pasta

25

Spotting game

Can you find all of these things in the book?

haddock

cupcake

strawberry

mushroom

pizza

grater

sushi

turkey

scales

salmon

colander

peas

milk tanker

crab

rolling pin

fusilli

radishes

whisk

apple tree

package of potato chips

Food quiz

Can you answer all of these questions about food? You can look back through the book to help you, if you like. The answers are on the last page.

1. Which of these foods are dairy products?

a) bread   b) butter   c) milk   d) jam   e) cheese

2. Which of these foods grow underground?

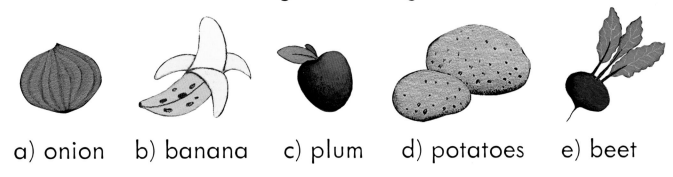

a) onion   b) banana   c) plum   d) potatoes   e) beet

3. Which of these foods do not come from the sea?

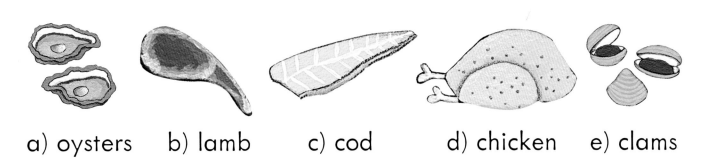

a) oysters   b) lamb   c) cod   d) chicken   e) clams

Shopping puzzle

Look at all the things in this shopping basket, then answer these questions:

1. Can you find two dairy foods?

2. How many fruits and vegetables are there altogether?

3. Which are there more of: cans of soup or jars of jam?

4. How many things are in the basket altogether?

The answers are on the last page.

Glossary

bake: cook foods such as bread and cakes in an oven.

baker: a person who bakes and sells bread and cakes.

bulb: the part of some plants that grows underground, and stores food for the plant.

butcher: a person who cuts up meat and sells it.

dairy food: food that comes from milk, such as cheese and yogurt.

farm: a place where a farmer grows food and keeps animals.

fisherman: a person who catches and sells fish.

flour: a fine powder made by grinding wheat grains.

fry: cook food in hot oil, usually in a shallow pan.

knead: squash and pull dough so that it becomes stretchy.

market: a place where people sell things from stalls.

oven: a machine with a door that you put food inside to cook.

paddy field: a field where rice plants are grown, which is kept covered in water.

pasta: a food made from flour mixed with salt and water or eggs, which comes in many different shapes.

root: the part of a plant that is below the ground, holds the plant in place, and takes up water and some food from the soil.

seafood: sea fish and other sea creatures that can be eaten.

stem: the long, thin part of a plant that grows up from the ground.

wheat: a type of grass grown in fields that can be made into food.

Index

Usborne Quicklinks

To visit websites with activities about food,
go to www.usborne.com/quicklinks and type
in the keywords "first book about food."
You'll find videos, games, recipes, and lots more.

Website researcher: Jacqui Clark

Answers

Jam jar puzzle
a) plums; b) cherries; c) strawberries; d) raspberries.

Spotting game
haddock p.16; cupcake p.15; strawberry p.6, 25; mushroom p.5; pizza p.24; grater p.23; sushi p.19;
turkey p.12; scales p.23; salmon p.16; colander p.23; peas p.5; milk tanker p.8; crab p.17;
rolling pin p.23; fusilli p.18; radishes p.4; whisk p.23; apple tree p.6, 7; package of potato chips p.22.

Food quiz
1. b, c, e; 2. a, d, e; 3. b, d.

Shopping puzzle
1. yogurt, milk; 2. 6; 3. jars of jam; 4. 15.